AF256154

rosie

hazyn forsythe

rosie liked to hop
where the grass was soft.

1

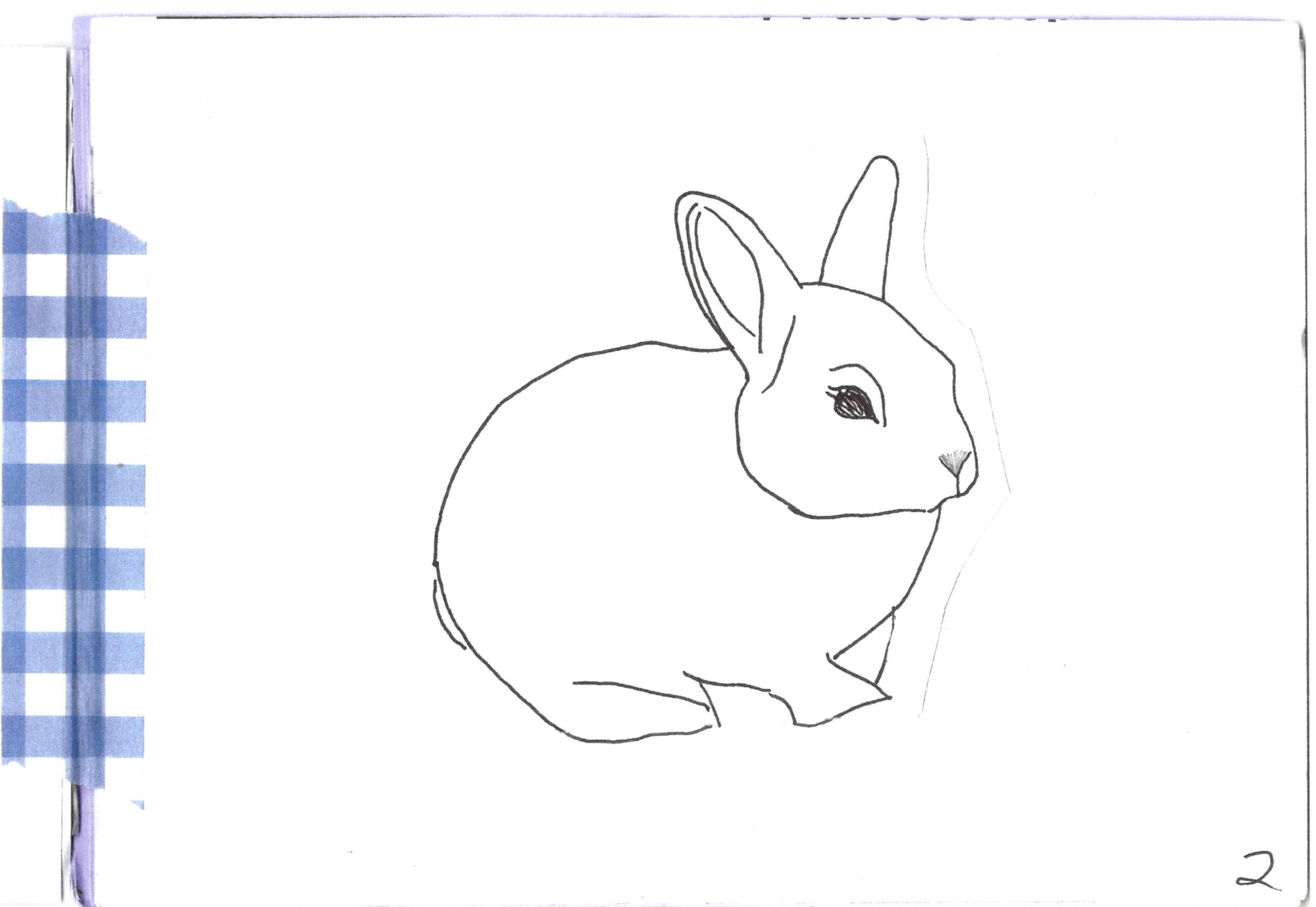

2

the air smelled sweet,
but not for long.
a bitter scent crept
through the grass—
old fruit left too long in
the sun, wet bark...
and something that
used to breathe.

rosie twitched her nose
and kept hopping.

3

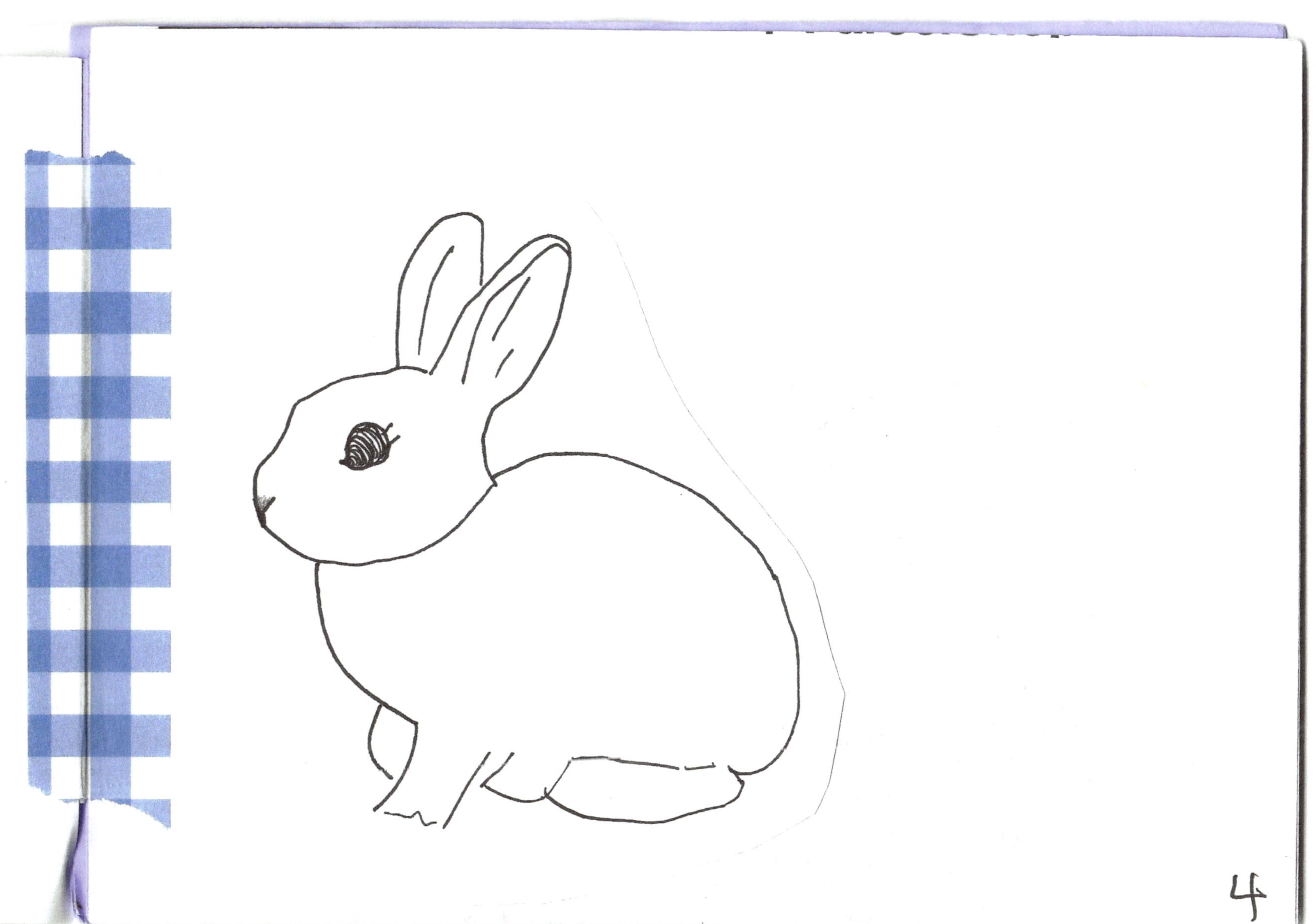

4

a low sound drifted across the field. not a bird, not the wind, not thunder.

it carried a groan that rose and fell like branches creaking in a very old tree.

rosie listened.

her ears tipped towards it, then away.

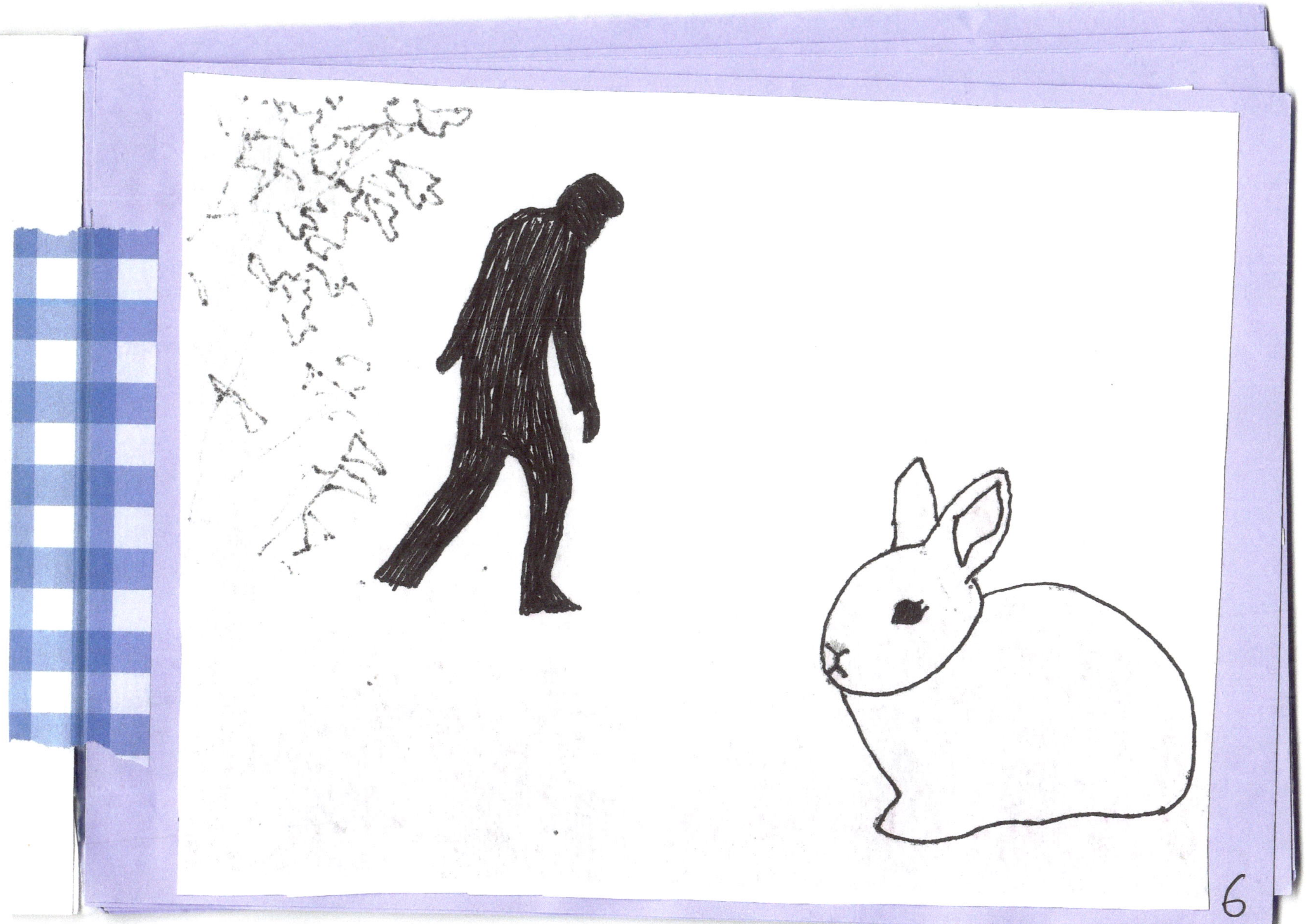

rosie froze.

her heart thudded fast.

the weeds stood tall, listening.

somewhere beyond them, the sound
stumbled closer. it was heavy and
slow, dragging the silence behind
it.

the air felt thick, sour,

wrong.

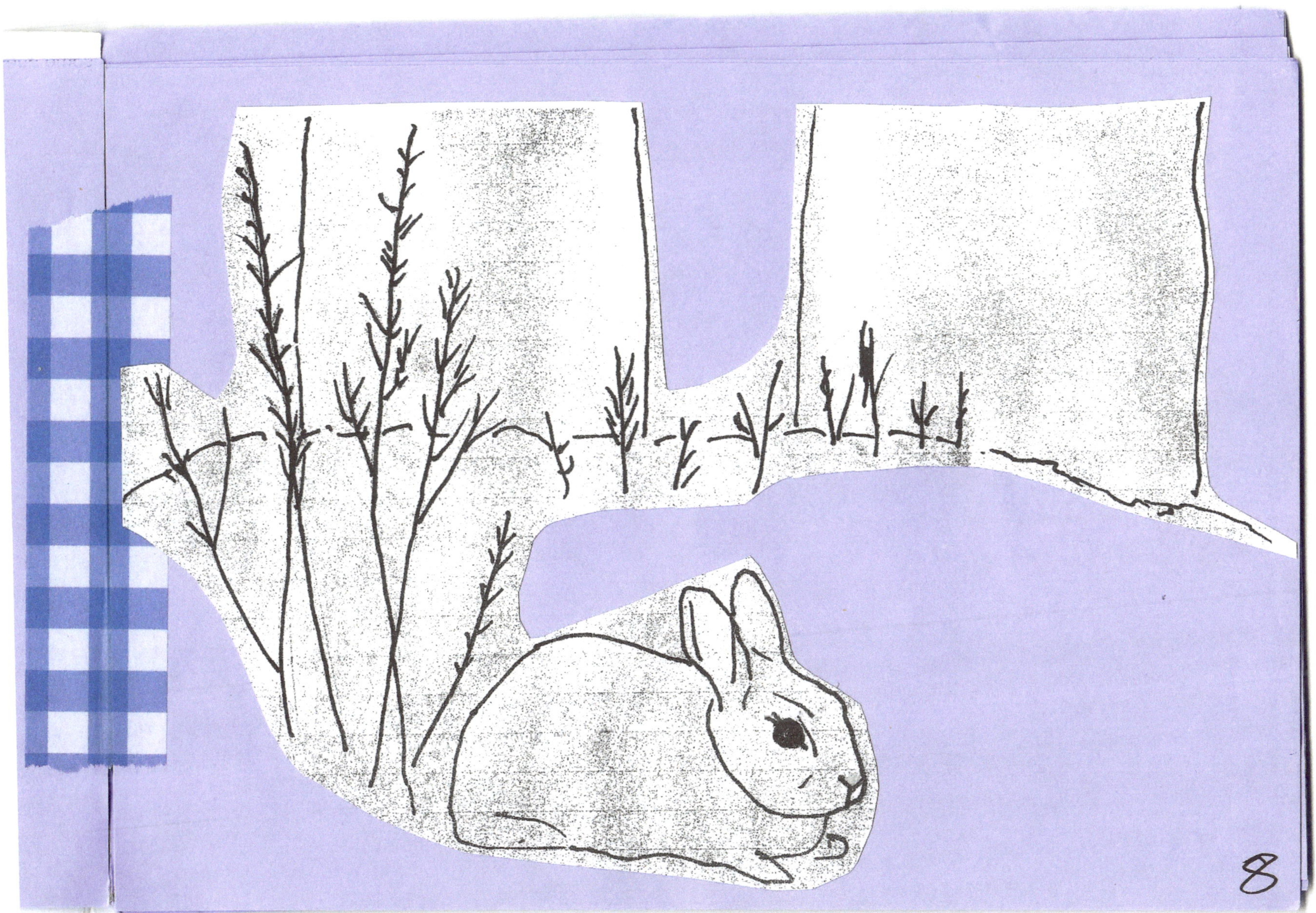

8

rosie pressed herself between
roots and stones.
the earth was cool and
smelled of safe things—
worms, moss, quiet time.

above her, something
big passed by, breathing in
whistles and huffs like
the wind through empty
rooms.

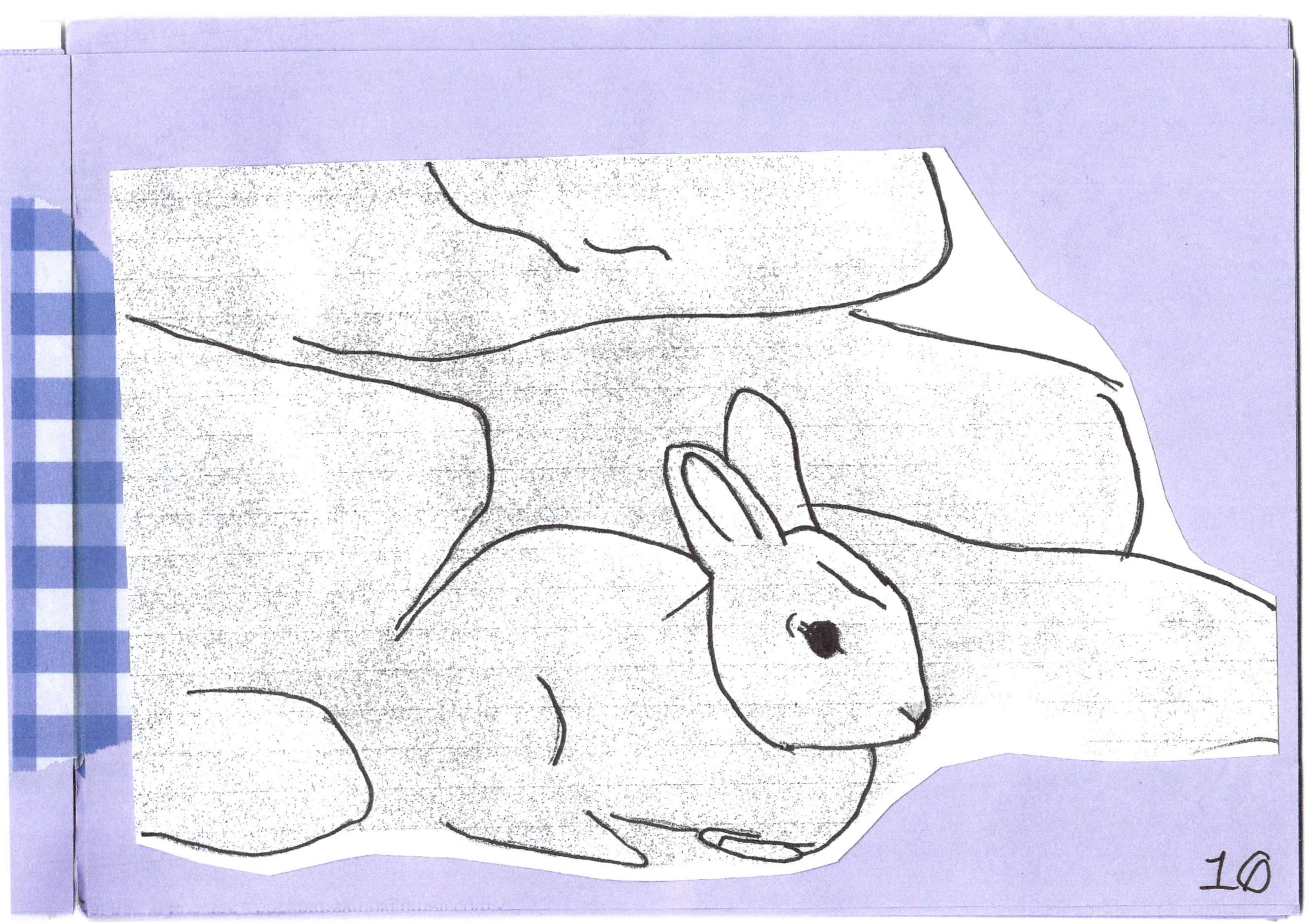

10

when the smell of rot thinned
and the groans were gone,
rosie lifted her head.

she brushed dust from
her fur, sniffed the wind
for the taste of water,
and hopped towards the
sound of small living things.

11

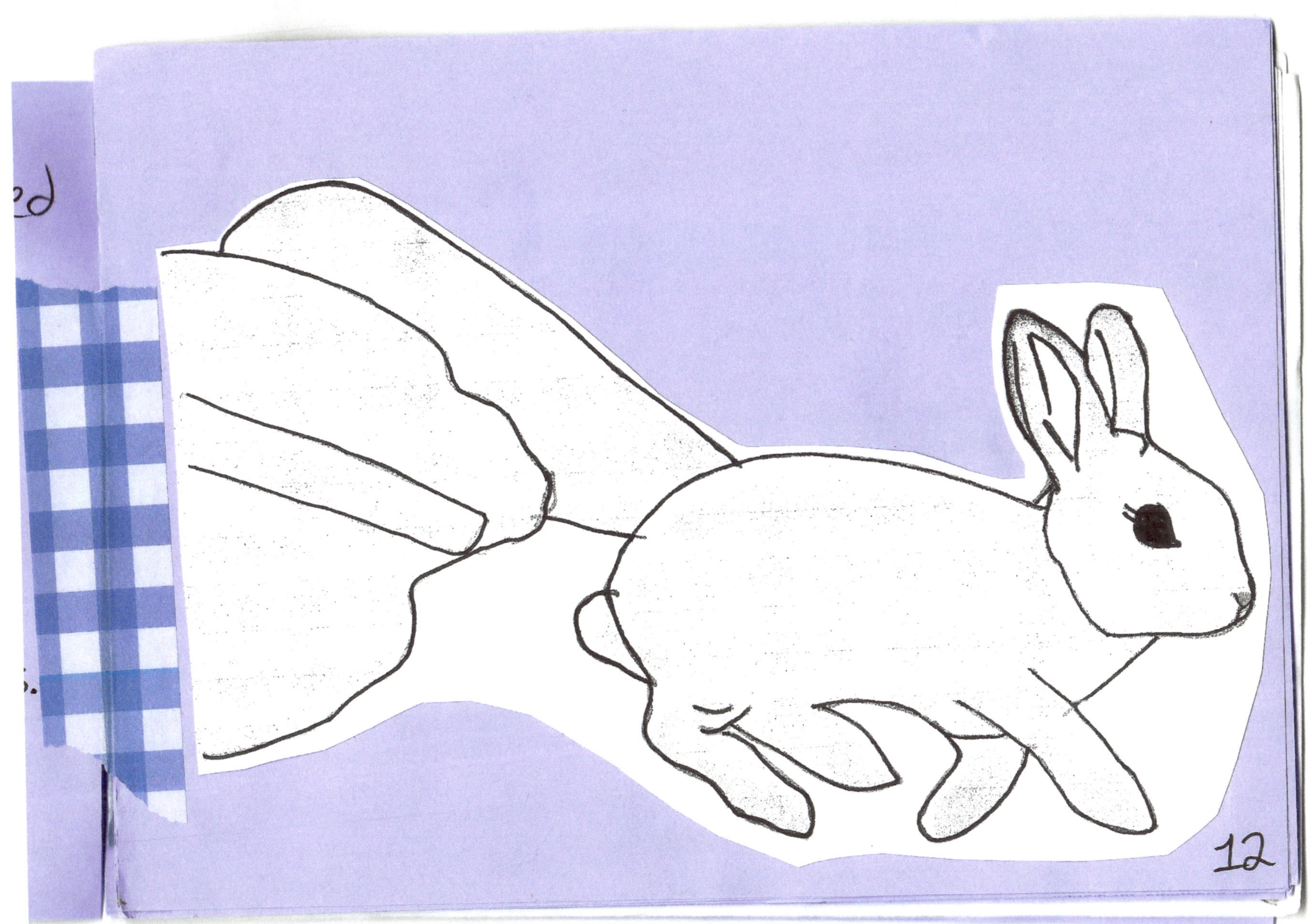

12

the sky turned golden
behind the broken things.

glass winked, trees grew
through fences, and (in the
hollows where soft shapes had
fallen), new flowers pushed
their faces to the light.

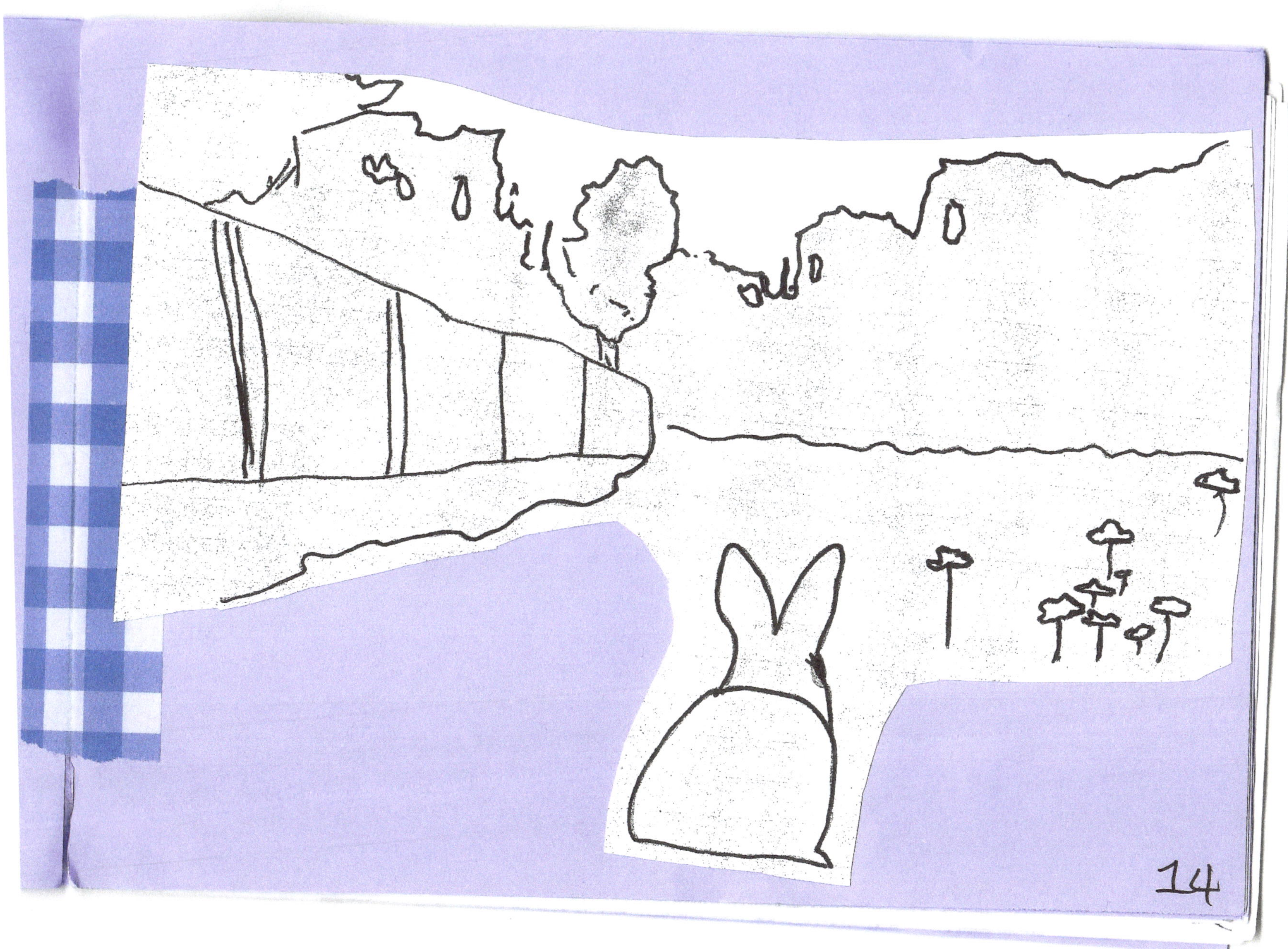

14

rosie found a patch
of clover and stayed a while.

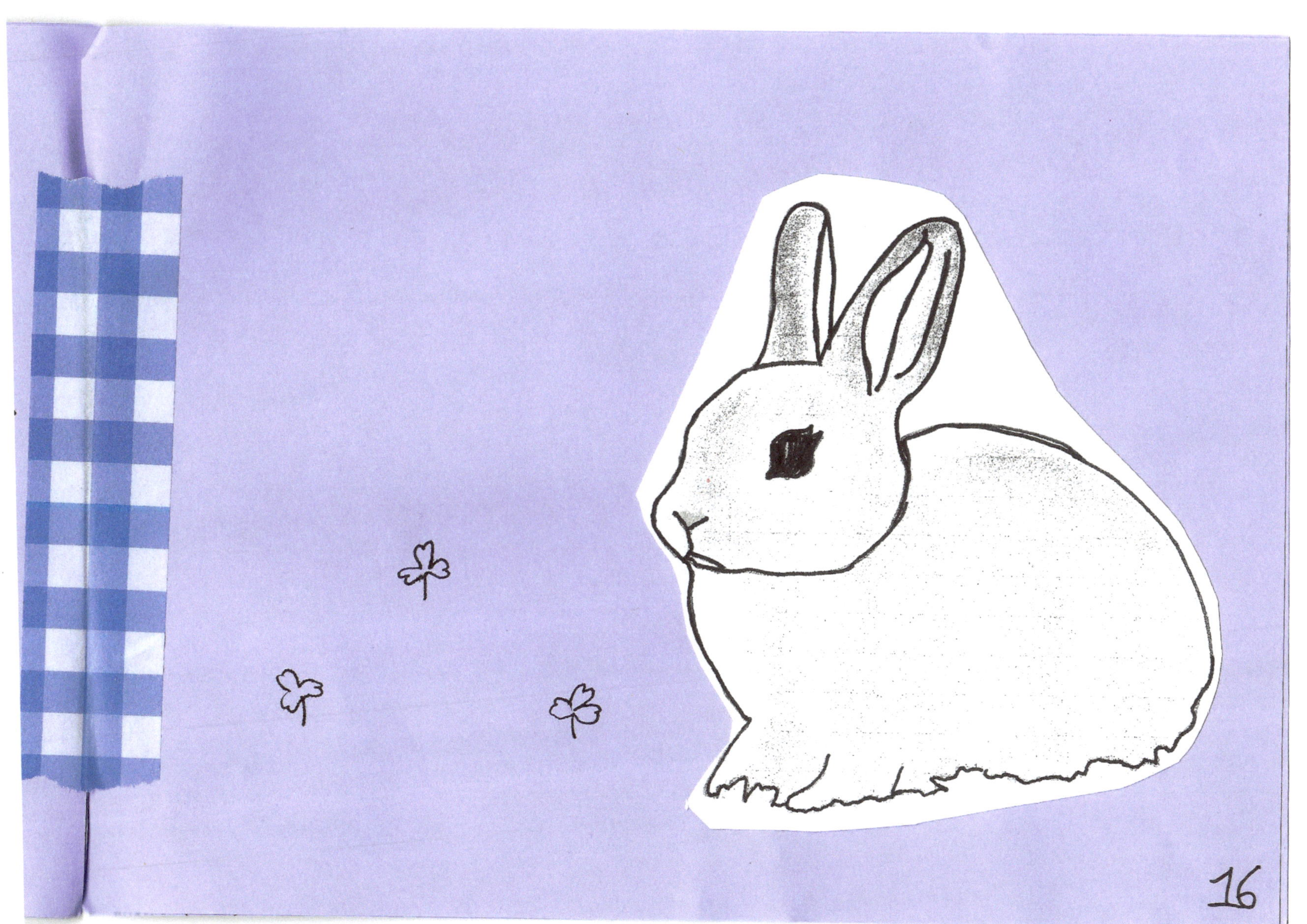

16

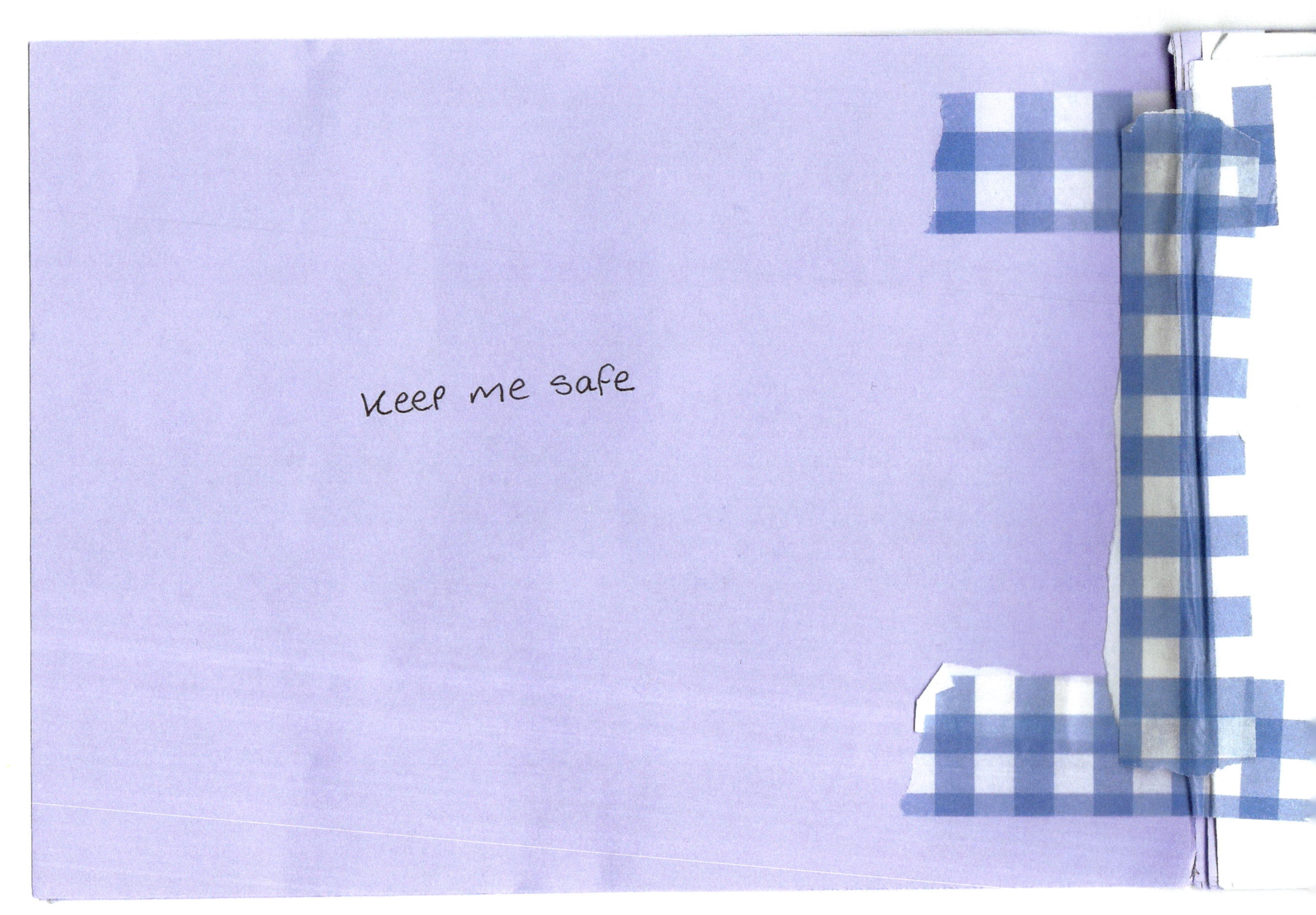
keep me safe